Samsung Galaxy Tab S6
User's Guide

Features, Setting up, Tips & Tricks and Troubleshooting of your Samsung Galaxy Tab S6

SCOTT DOWNING

Goodwater Publishing
279 Stoney Lane
Dallas, TX 75212
Texas
USA

Copyright © 2019 Scott Downing
All rights reserved. Except for the quotation of short passages for the purposes of criticism and review, no part of this publication may be reproduced, stored in a retrieval system, or transmitted, in any form or by any means, electronic, mechanical, photocopying, recording or otherwise, without the prior written permission of the publisher or a license from the Copyright Licensing Agency Limited.

CONTENTS

CONTENTS	i
INTRODUCTION	1
SAMSUNG GALAXY TAB S4, S5e AND S6 COMPARISON	1
GETTING STARTED	6
DEVICE LAYOUT	6
CHARGING THE BATTERY	6
TURNING THE DEVICE ON AND OFF	7
INITIAL SETTING UP OF GALAXY TAB S6	8
SET UP AND MANAGE YOUR SAMSUNG ACCOUNT	8
TRANSFERRING DATA FROM YOUR PREVIOUS DEVICE (SMART SWITCH)	9
NAVIGATING GALAXY TAB S6	10
HOME SCREEN AND APPS SCREEN	12
LOCK OR UNLOCK YOUR DEVICE'S SCREEN	14
NOTIFICATION PANEL	15
APPS AND FEATURES	17
S PEN FEATURES	17
BIXBY	26
PHONE	29

CREATING AND MANAGING CONTACTS ON THE DEVICE	33
MESSAGES	35
INTERNET	36
CAMERA	37
GALLERY	39
MULTI WINDOW	41
SAMSUNG NOTES	43
SAMSUNG FLOW	46
MY FILES	47
SMARTTHINGS	47
SAMSUNG DeX	50
SETTINGS	54
CONNECTIONS	54
PRINTING	57
DISPLAY	58
LOCK SCREEN	60
ACCOUNTS AND BACKUP	63
SAMSUNG GALAXY TAB S6 TIPS & TRICKS	67
TROUBLESHOOTINGPROBLEMS WITH GALAXY TAB S6	71

iv

INTRODUCTION

With the official announcement of Galaxy Tab S6 in July 2019, Samsung launched a high-end Android tablet that's designed for both productivity work and entertainment. The Galaxy Tab S6 sits at the top Samsung's current Android tablet range, which includes the low-end Galaxy Tab A and the midrange Galaxy Tab 5e released earlier this year.

The Galaxy Tab S6 runs on Android 9 Pie with version 1.5 of Samsung's OneUI interface. It also has multitasking support for DeX interface, which provides a more laptop-like experience when using the tablet with a keyboard. The new Book Cover keyboard attachment has a function to launch DeX quickly. DeX can also be outputted to an external display using the Galaxy Tab S6's USB Type-C port.

The S Pen stylus (a Bluetooth-enabled remote functionality) usually found alongside the Galaxy Note series is included for the first time in the Galaxy Tab S6. The S-Pen can now take selfies and videos, as well as scroll through media — all without touching your tablet, up to a range of about 10 meters. This is called Air Actions and, for example, you can switch camera modes just by pressing and holding the S Pen button and waving your hand left or right without touching the tablet.

This guide will assist you with all of the features and functionality of your Galaxy Tab S6. It also contains a lot of hidden tips and tricks to help you make the most out of your Galaxy Tab S6.

SAMSUNG GALAXY TAB S4, S5e AND S6 COMPARISON

All three of Samsung's tablets have a lot in common, but dig deeper, and there are some differences worth noting. The specs for both tablets are compared side-by-side in the table below. The Tablets' processor performance, battery life, charging, design, and durability are also compared here. Among the most notable upgrades here are the Bluetooth S Pen and the considerably higher horsepower; as a result, the Snapdragon 855 chipset. The Galaxy Tab S6 has a dual-camera on-board and fingerprint sensor under the display.

Specifications

	Samsung Galaxy Tab S6	Samsung Galaxy Tab S5e	Samsung Galaxy Tab S4
Size	244.5 x 159.5 x 5.7 mm (9.62 x 6.28 x 0.22 inches)	245 x 160 x 5.5 mm (9.64 x 6.29 x 0.21 inches)	249.3 x 164.3 x 7.1 mm (9.81 x 6.47 x 0.28 inches)
Weight	420 grams (0.92 pounds)	400 grams (0.88 pounds)	482 grams (1.06 pounds)
Screen size	10.5-inch Super AMOLED	10.5-inch Super AMOLED	10.5-inch Super AMOLED
Screen resolution	2,560 x 1,600 pixels (287 pixels-per-inch)	2,560 x 1,600 pixels (287 pixels-per-inch)	2,560 x 1,600 pixels (287 pixels-per-inch)
Operating system	Android 9.0 (Pie)	Android 9.0 (Pie)	Android 9.0 (Pie)
Storage space	128GB, 256GB	64GB, 128GB	64GB, 256GB
MicroSD card slot	Yes	Yes	Yes
Processor	Qualcomm Snapdragon 855	Qualcomm Snapdragon 670	Qualcomm Snapdragon 835
RAM (Expandable to)	6GB (8GB)	4GB (6GB)	4GB
Camera	13MP and 5MP rear, 8MP front	13MP rear, 8MP front	13MP rear, 8MP front
Video	2,160p at 30fps	2,160p at 30fps	2,160p at 30fps
Ports	USB-C	USB-C	USB-C, 3.5mm audio jack
Fingerprint sensor	Yes (in-display)	Yes (side)	No

| Battery | 7,040mAh | 7,040mAh | 7,300mAh |

Processor performance, battery life and charging

The Samsung Galaxy Tab S4 has a Snapdragon 835 processor inside, which was the best chip available a couple of years ago. The Galaxy Tab S5e has a newer chip, but it's a midrange Snapdragon 670. There's very little difference in how these processors perform, but the 835 was faster than the 670 in most circumstances before the advent of the Galaxy Tab S6. The Galaxy Tab S6 on arrival blew them away entirely with the Snapdragon 855, which offers 80% more processing power. The newer tablet also promises faster graphics and boasts optimized gaming Artificial Intelligence.

In terms of battery life, the Tab S4 has a clear edge in lasting strength with more than 200mAh of extra battery capacity. All three can be charged quickly at up 18W, so there's no dividing them on charging speed.

Design and durability

All of these tablets are adeptly made, and they each have a touch of luxurious style about them. Both the Galaxy Tab S6 and S5e are much slimmer and lighter than S4, which makes them easier to hold one-handed. They also have a convenient fingerprint sensor and something most people are used to; compared to the iris scanner in the Galaxy Tab S4, which is not easy to use.

The Galaxy Tab S6 gets the edge with a more exciting choice of colors and better accessory integration. The S Pen attaches magnetically, and there's a much-improved keyboard case with a trackpad.

Camera

While the competition to release the best camera phone is fierce, it's something of an afterthought with tablets. That said, the Tab S4 and Tab S5e sport a respectable pairing of a 13-megapixel main shooter and an 8-megapixel front-facing camera that's ideal for video calls. The Tab S6 kicks things up a notch with a dual lens main camera that pairs a 13-megapixel lens with a secondary 5-megapixel wide-angle lens, which offers a 123-degree field of view. It also has an 8-megapixel front-facing camera.

S Pen

There is a standout feature that only the Galaxy Tab S4 and S6 have — the S Pen. If you like to use a stylus, make handwritten notes, or sketch on your tablet, then the S Pen is a big reason to choose the Galaxy Tab S6 over the Tab S5e. The new S Pen that comes with the Galaxy Tab S6 also offers remote control functionality and charges wirelessly when attached magnetically to the back of the Galaxy Tab S6. After about 10 minutes of charge, the S Pen will be able to work for a whopping 10 hours. The remote control features include S Pen Air, allowing the accessory to snap selfies and videos remotely, or control movies without the tablet even being in your possession.

Improved version of Samsung DeX and Book Cover Keyboard

Samsung DeX is not hardware — it's a platform that extends your smartphone into a desktop computing experience. The Samsung Galaxy Tab S6 has an improved version of Samsung DeX built into it, giving you an instant and seamless transition to a laptop-like experience, so you can easily multitask and optimize your viewing experience.

The tablet's new dedicated Book Cover Keyboard has a DeX function key that can launch DeX with a tap using a keyboard shortcut (**Fn** + **DeX**).

This DeX mode is enabled in the Galaxy Tab S6 when a connection is made by snapping the Book Cover keyboard onto the Pogo connector on the left side of the device. The new Keyboard also has a trackpad so you don't need to connect a separate wireless mouse.

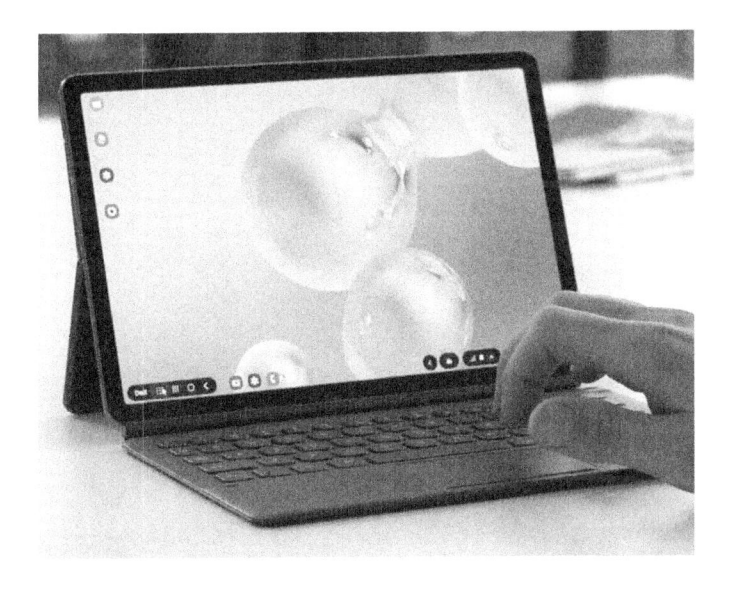

GETTING STARTED

DEVICE LAYOUT

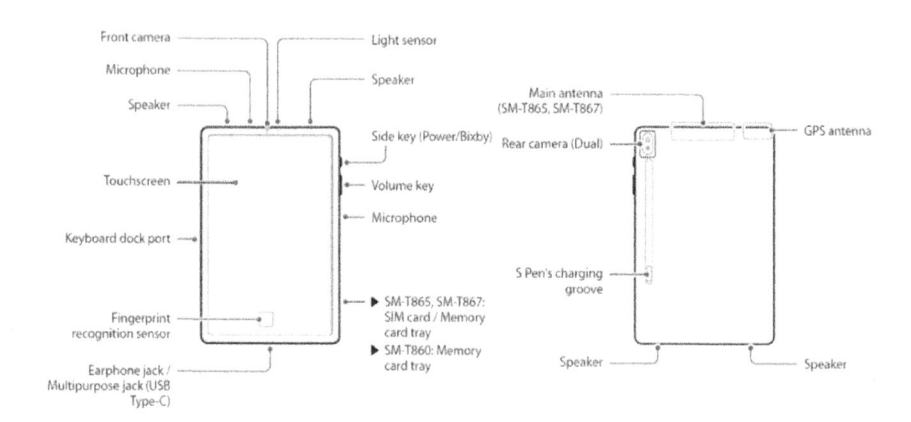

```
Front camera
Microphone
Speaker                    Light sensor
                           Speaker
                                          Main antenna
                                          (SM-T865, SM-T867)
                           Side key (Power/Bixby)                    GPS antenna
Touchscreen                                Rear camera (Dual)
                           Volume key
                           Microphone
Keyboard dock port
                                          S Pen's charging
                                          groove
Fingerprint                ▶ SM-T865, SM-T867:
recognition sensor           SIM card / Memory
                             card tray
                           ▶ SM-T860: Memory
Earphone jack /              card tray          Speaker              Speaker
Multipurpose jack (USB
Type-C)
```

CHARGING THE BATTERY

It's very important that you charge the battery before using it for the first time or when it has been unused for extended periods. Always use only Samsung-approved battery, charger, and cable specifically designed for your device. Incompatible battery, charger, and cable can cause serious injuries or damage to your device. Use only USB Type-C cable supplied with the device. The device may be damaged if you use Micro USB cable. Follow the steps below to charge your Galaxy Tab S6.

1. Connect the USB cable to the USB power adaptor.
2. Plug the USB cable into the device's multipurpose jack.
3. Plug the USB power adaptor into an electric socket.
4. After fully charging, disconnect the charger from the device. Then, unplug the charger from the electric socket.

Fast charging

The Galaxy Tab S6 has a built-in fast charging feature. You can charge the battery more quickly while the device or its screen is turned off.

Follow the following steps to activate the fast charging feature:

1. Go to the **Settings** app
2. Tap **Device care** and select **Battery**
3. Tap ⋮ and select **Settings**
4. Tap the **Fast cable charging** switch to activate it.

TURNING THE DEVICE ON AND OFF

Turning the device on

Press and hold the Side key for a few seconds to turn on the device.

When you turn on your device for the first time or after performing a data reset, follow the on-screen instructions to set up your device.

Turning the device off

1. To turn off the device, press and hold the Side key and the Volume Down key simultaneously. Alternatively, open the notification panel and tap 🔘 **Power Off**.
2. To restart the device, press and hold the Side key and the Volume Down key simultaneously and tap 🔘 **Restart**.

You can set the device to turn off when you press and hold only the side key. Follow these steps below:

1. Launch the **Settings** app
2. Tap **Advanced features** and select **Side key**
3. Tap **Power off menu** under **Press and hold**

INITIAL SETTING UP OF GALAXY TAB S6

When you turn on your device for the first time or after performing a data reset, follow the on-screen instructions to set up your device.

1. Press and hold the Side key for a few seconds to turn on the device.
2. Select your preferred device language and select
3. Follow the on-screen instructions to complete the setup and the Home screen will appear.

SET UP AND MANAGE YOUR SAMSUNG ACCOUNT

Your Samsung account is an integrated account service that allows you to use a variety of Samsung services provided by mobile devices, TVs, and the Samsung website. If you do not have a Samsung account, you should create one. You can create a Samsung account using your email address by following the steps below.

1. Launch the **Settings** app and tap **Accounts and backup**
2. Select **Accounts**
3. Select **Add account** and tap on **Samsung account**.
4. Tap **Create account**.
5. Follow the on-screen instructions to complete creating your account.

Signing in to your Samsung account

If you already have a Samsung account, sign in to your Samsung account.

1. Go to **Settings** and tap
2. Enter your Samsung account ID and password and tap **Sign in**.

3. Follow the on-screen instructions to complete signing in to your Samsung account.

TRANSFERRING DATA FROM YOUR PREVIOUS DEVICE (SMART SWITCH)

Use Smart Switch to transfer contacts, photos, music, videos, messages, notes, calendars, and more from your old device. Smart Switch can transfer your data via USB cable, Wi-Fi, or computer.

Transferring data wirelessly

Transfer data from your previous device to your device wirelessly via Wi-Fi Direct.

1. On the previous device, launch **Smart Switch**. If you do not have the app, download it from Galaxy Store.
2. On your device, launch the **Settings** app and tap **Accounts and backup**, then select **Smart Switch**.
3. Place the devices near each other.
4. On the previous device, tap **Send data** and select **Wireless**.
5. On the previous device, select an item to transfer and tap **Send**.
6. On your device, tap **Receive**.
7. Follow the on-screen instructions to transfer data from your previous device.

Backing up and restoring data using external storage

Transfer data using external storage, such as a microSD card.

1. Back up data from your previous device to external storage.
2. Insert or connect the external storage device to your device.

3. On your device, launch the **Settings** app and tap **Accounts and backup** and select **Smart Switch**.
4. Click on ▦ and select **Restore**.
5. Follow the on-screen instructions to transfer data from external storage.

NAVIGATING GALAXY TAB S6

The Galaxy Tab S6 comes with a touch screen that responds best to a light touch from your finger or the S Pen. Using excessive pressure or any sharp object on the touch screen may damage the touchscreen and void the warranty.

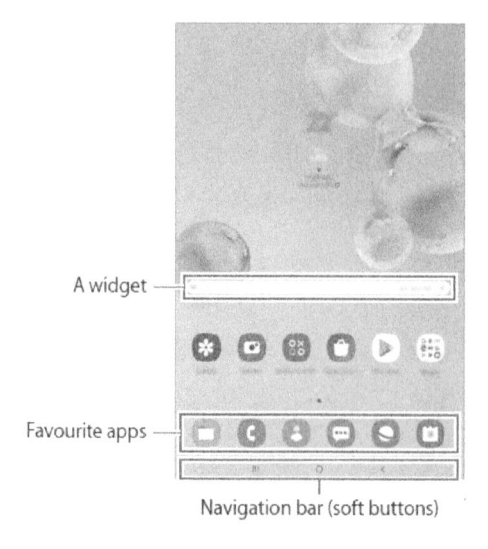

A widget

Favourite apps

Navigation bar (soft buttons)

Navigation bar (soft buttons)

When you turn on the screen, the soft buttons will appear on the navigation bar at the bottom of the screen. The soft buttons are set to the Recents button, Home button, and Back button by default. The functions of the buttons can change according to the app currently being used or usage environment. The functions of the navigation bar soft buttons include:

- Recents — Tap to open the list of recent apps.
- Home Button — Tap to return to the Home screen and also tap and hold to launch the Google Assistant app.
- Back — Tap to return to the previous screen.

Hiding the navigation bar

You can hide the navigation bar in order to view files or use apps on a wider screen. This can be achieved by following the steps below:

1. Go to **Settings and** tap **Display**
2. Select **Navigation bar**, and then tap **Full screen gestures** under **Navigation type**.

The navigation bar will be hidden and the gesture hints will appear where the soft buttons are located. To use the soft buttons, drag the gesture hint of the desired button upwards. If you want to hide the gesture hints at the bottom of the screen, tap the **Gesture hints** switch to deactivate it.

HOME SCREEN AND APPS SCREEN

The Home screen is the starting point for accessing all of the device's features. It displays widgets, shortcuts to apps, and more. While the Apps screen displays icons for all apps, including newly installed apps.

Switching between Home and Apps screens

On the Home screen, swipe upwards or downwards to open the Apps screen. To return to the Home screen, swipe upwards or downwards on the Apps screen. Alternatively, tap the Home button or the Back button.

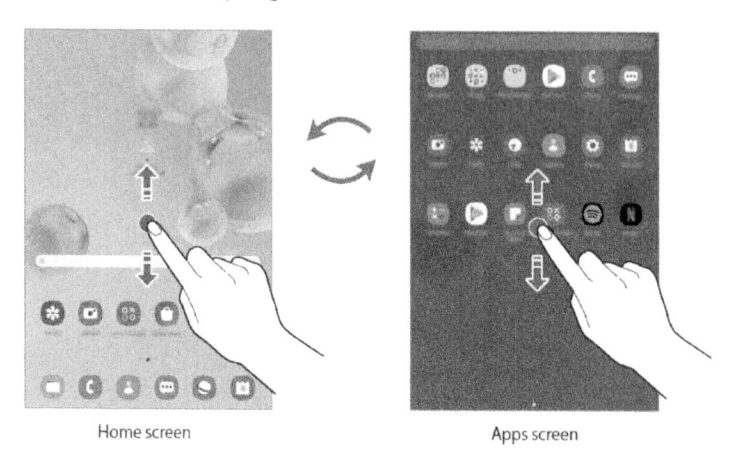

Home screen   Apps screen

If you add the Apps button on the Home screen,
You can open the Apps screen by tapping the Apps button shortcut on the Home screen. The following steps will help you add the Apps button shortcut on the Home screen.
1. On the Home screen, tap and hold an empty area.
2. Tap **Home screen settings**, and then select the Apps button switch to activate it.
3. The **Apps button** will be added at the bottom of the Home screen.

Apps button

Editing the Home screen

On the Home screen, tap and hold an empty area, or pinch your fingers together to access the editing options. You can set the wallpaper, add widgets, and more. You can also add, delete, or rearrange Home screen panels.

- **Adding panels**: Swipe to the left, and then tap **circled +** button.
- **Moving panels**: Tap and hold a panel preview, and then drag it to a new location.
- **Deleting panels**: Tap **Delete** button on the panel.
- **Wallpapers**: Change the wallpaper settings for the Home screen and the locked screen.
- **Widgets**: Widgets are small apps that launch specific app functions to provide information and convenient access on your Home screen. Tap and hold a widget, and then drag it to the Home screen. The widget will be added on the Home screen.
- **Home screen settings**: Configure settings for the Home screen, such as the screen grid or layout.

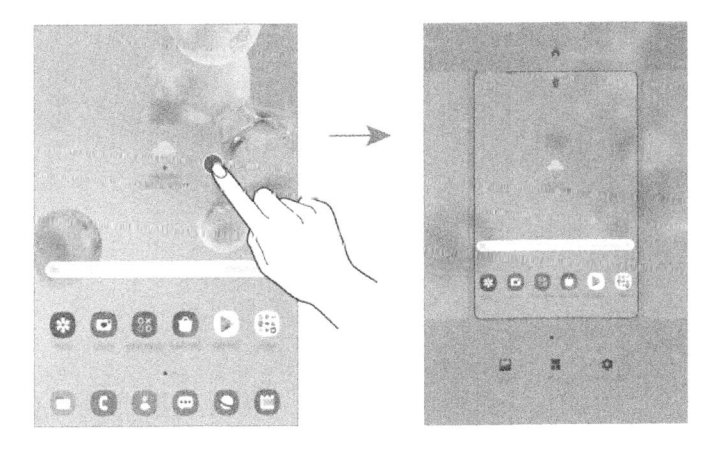

Displaying all apps on the Home screen

Without using a separate Apps screen, you can set the device to display all apps on the Home screen. All apps can be displayed on the home screen in the following way.

1. On the Home screen, tap and hold an empty area.
2. Tap **Home screen settings** and select **Home screen layout**
3. Select **Home screen only** and click **Apply**.

You can now access all your apps by swiping to the left on the Home screen.

LOCK OR UNLOCK YOUR DEVICE'S SCREEN

Pressing the Side key turns off the screen and locks it. Also, the screen turns off and automatically locks if the device is not used for a specified period. To unlock the screen, swipe in any direction when the screen turns on. If the screen is off, press the Side key to turn on the screen or alternatively, double-tap the screen.

Locked screen

Changing the screen lock method

To change the screen lock method, follow the steps below:

1. Launch the **Settings** app and tap **Lock screen**
2. Tap **Screen lock type** and select a method.

When you set a pattern, PIN, password, or your biometric data for the screen lock method, you can protect your personal information by preventing others from accessing your device. After setting the screen lock method, the device will require an unlock code whenever unlocking it.

- **Swipe**: Swipe in any direction on the screen to unlock it.
- **Pattern**: Draw a pattern with four or more dots to unlock the screen.
- **PIN**: Enter a PIN with at least four numbers to unlock the screen.
- **Password**: Enter a password with at least four characters, numbers, or symbols to unlock the screen.
- **None**: Do not set a screen lock method.
- **Face**: Register your face to unlock the screen.
- **Fingerprints**: Register your fingerprints to unlock the screen.

NOTIFICATION PANEL

When you receive new notifications, indicator icons appear on the status bar. To see more information about the icons, open the notification panel and view the details. To open the notification panel, drag the status bar downwards. To close the notification panel, swipe upwards on the screen. You can use the following functions on the notification panel.

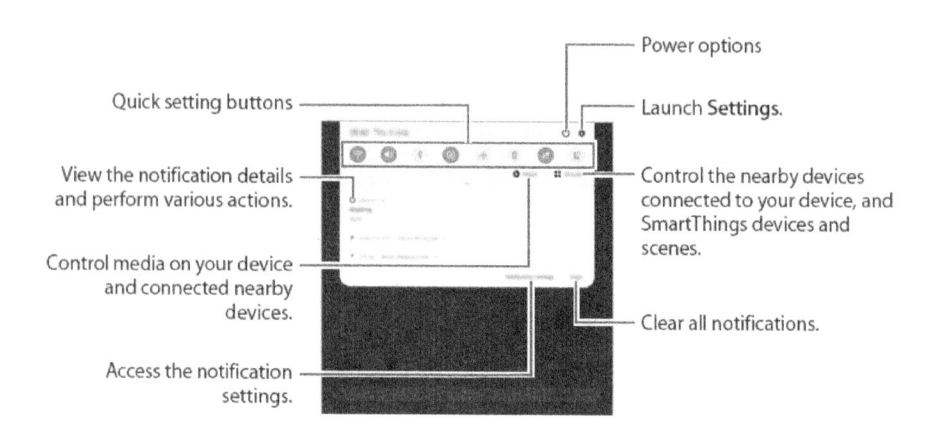

Quick setting buttons —
View the notification details and perform various actions.
Control media on your device and connected nearby devices.
Access the notification settings.

Power options
Launch **Settings**.
Control the nearby devices connected to your device, and SmartThings devices and scenes.
Clear all notifications.

Using quick setting buttons

Tap quick setting buttons to activate certain features. Swipe downwards on the notification panel to view more buttons.

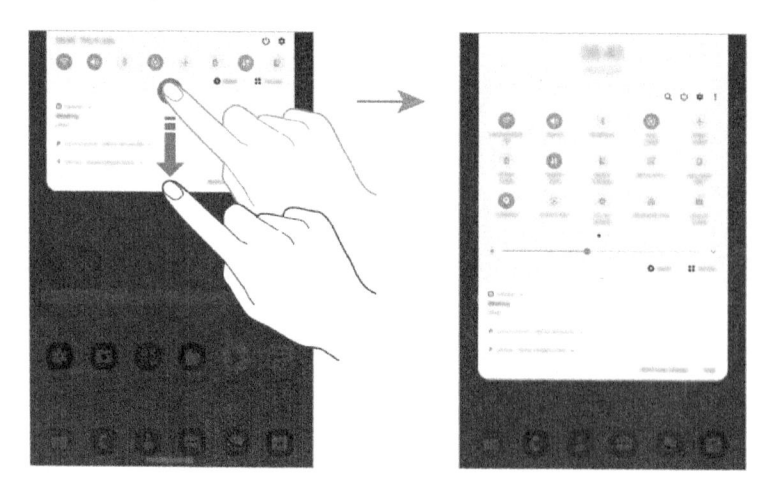

APPS AND FEATURES

Installing apps

Apps may be purchased and downloaded from either Galaxy or play Store. To install, launch the Galaxy or Play Store app. Browse apps by category or search for apps by keyword. Select an app to view information about it. To download free apps, tap **INSTALL**. To purchase and download apps where charges apply, tap the price and follow the on-screen instructions.

Uninstalling or disabling apps

Tap and hold an app and select an option.

- **Uninstall**: Uninstall downloaded apps.
- **Disable**: Disable selected default apps that cannot be uninstalled from the device.

Enabling apps

1. Launch the **Settings** app and tap Apps
2. Click on the **Down Arrow** and select **Disabled**.
3. Select an app and then tap **Enable**.

S PEN FEATURES

Air actions

Control apps remotely by using the S Pen connected to your device via Bluetooth Low Energy (BLE). For example, you can quickly launch apps, such as the camera app, by pressing and holding the S Pen button. Also, while using the camera app, you can take a photo by pressing the button once. While playing music, you can turn the volume up if you lift the S Pen up while pressing and holding the S Pen button and turn the volume down if you lower it.

The Air Action can be activated in the following ways:

1. Launch the **Settings** app and tap **Advanced features**.
2. Click on **S Pen** and select **Air actions**.
3. Tap the switch to activate the feature.

Taking photos with the S Pen

Even though you take photos with your device placing for a distance, you can easily take photos by pressing the S Pen button without setting a timer.

1. Launch the **Camera** app.
2. Press the S Pen button once to take a photo.
   - To change the shooting mode, move the S Pen to the left or right while pressing and holding the S Pen button.
   - To switch between cameras, press the S Pen button twice.

Changing apps or features to use

Change the app, feature, or actions you want to use with the S Pen feature. To change the app to launch, open the Air action setting screen, tap **Hold down Pen button to**, and then select an app or feature.

To change actions for each app, open the Air action setting screen and select an app under **App actions**. You can change actions by tapping items under **Pen button** or **Gestures**.

Connecting another S Pen

Before using S Pen features with another S Pen, such as Air action, you must connect the S Pen to your device.

1. Attach the S Pen to the S Pen's charging groove.

2. Open the notification panel, tap **S Pen air actions** icon and then tap again to reactivate it.

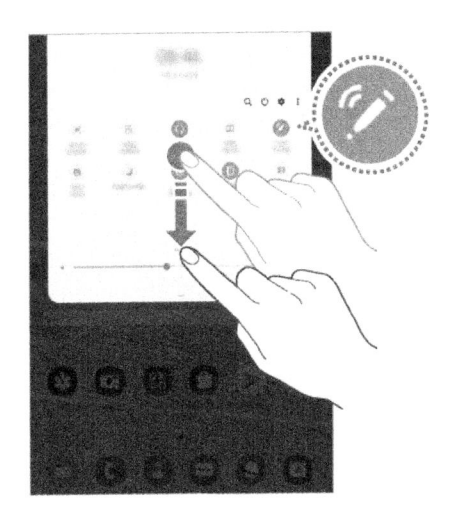

3. Tap **Connect new S Pen**. S Pen will be connected. You may experience a brief delay before it finishes connecting.

You can only connect Samsung-approved S Pens that support Bluetooth Low Energy (BLE). Do not detach the S Pen from the device when it is being connected. Doing so will interrupt the process. If it fails to connect or you want to use the previous S Pen, reconnect it with the method shown above.

Resetting your S Pen

If the S Pen has connection problems or the S Pen disconnects often, reset the S Pen and connect it again. Attach the S Pen to the S Pen's charging groove. Then, open the Air action setting screen and tap ⋮ and select **Reset S Pen**.

Air command

Air command is a menu that provides S Pen features and quick access to frequently used apps. To open the Air command panel, hover the S Pen over the screen and press the S Pen button. You can also tap the Air command icon with the S Pen. Drag upwards or downwards on the Air command panel and select a function or app you want. When the screen is off or locked with a screen lock method, removing the S Pen will not open the Air command panel.

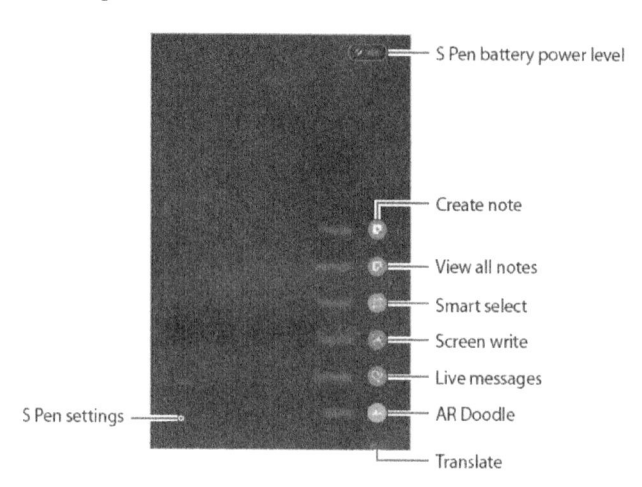

- S Pen battery power level
- Create note
- View all notes
- Smart select
- Screen write
- Live messages
- S Pen settings
- AR Doodle
- Translate

Air command icon

When the Air command panel is closed, the Air command icon will remain on the screen. You can open the Air command panel by tapping the icon with the S Pen. If the Air command icon does not appear on the screen, follow the steps to activate it.

1. Launch the **Settings** app and tap **Advanced features**
2. Click on **S Pen** and tap the **Floating** icon switch to activate it.

While using apps that support the Air action feature, you can view actions available with each app by hovering the S Pen over the Air command icon.

Adding shortcuts to the Air command panel

Some of the various S Pen features can be activated from the Air command panel. The shortcuts that do not appear on the panel by default can be added by using the Add shortcuts feature. On the Air command panel, tap **Add shortcuts** and select apps or functions to open from the panel. The S Pen features include:

- **Create note**: Create notes easily in a pop-up window without launching the **Samsung Notes** app.
- **View all notes**: View all notes in the **Samsung Notes** app.
- **Smart select**: Use the S Pen to select an area and perform actions, such as sharing or saving.
- **Screen write**: Capture screenshots to write or draw on them or crop an area from the captured image. You can also capture the current content and the hidden content on an elongated page, such as a webpage.
- **Live messages**: Instead of text message, create and send a unique message by recording your actions while handwriting or drawing a live message and saving it as an animated file.
- **AR Doodle**: Record fun videos with virtual handwriting or drawings on faces.
- **Translate**: Hover the S Pen over a word to translate it.
- **PENUP**: Post your artwork, view others' artwork, and get useful drawing tips.
- **Bixby Vision**: Use the Bixby Vision features to search for similar images, detect and translate text, and more.
- **Magnify**: Hover the S Pen over an area of the screen to enlarge it.
- **Glance**: Reduce an app to a thumbnail and hover the S Pen over the thumbnail to open the app in full screen view.

- **Colouring**: Add colours to images provided by PENUP using the S Pen.
- **Write on calendar**: Launch the Calendar app and write or draw on the screen.
- **Add shortcuts**: Add shortcuts to frequently used apps to the Air command panel.

Create note

Create notes easily in a pop-up window without launching the **Samsung Notes** app.

1. Open the Air command panel and tap **Create note**. Alternatively, double-tap the screen while pressing and holding the S Pen button. The note screen will appear as a pop-up window.
2. Create a note using the S Pen.
3. When you are finished composing the note, tap **Save**. The note will be saved in **Samsung Notes**.

Smart select

Use the S Pen to select an area and perform actions, such as sharing or saving. You can also select an area from a video and capture it as a GIF animation.

1. When there is content you want to capture, such as a part of an image, open the Air command panel and tap **Smart select**.
2. Select a desired shape icon on the toolbar and drag the S Pen across the content you want to select.
3. Select an option to use with the selected area.
    - **Extract text**: Extract text from the selected area.
    - **Pin to screen**: Pin the selected area to the screen.

- ⌕ : Automatically changes the appearance of the selected area.
- ✏ : Write or draw on the selected area.
- ⊲ : Share the selected area with others.
- ⬇ : Save the selected area in **Gallery**.

Capturing an area from a video

While playing a video, select an area and capture it as a GIF animation.

1. When there is content you want to capture during video playback, open the Air command panel and tap **Smart select**.
2. On the toolbar, tap GIF
3. Adjust the position and size of the capturing area.

Adjust the position.
Drag a corner of the frame to resize.
Select a quality.

4. Make sure that the video is playing before capturing a video. Then tap **Record** to start capturing but note that the audio will not be recorded.
5. Tap Stop to stop capturing.
6. Select an option to use with the selected area.
    - ✏ : Write or draw on the selected area. Tap ▶ to view the result before saving the file.

- ![share icon] : Share the selected area with others.
- ![save icon] : Save the selected area in Gallery.

Live messages

Instead of a text message, create and send a unique message by recording your actions while handwriting or drawing a live message and saving it as an animated file.

1. When you want to send an animated message while composing a message, open the Air command panel and tap **Live messages**. The live message window will appear.
2. Customize background image and tap **Done** or **Start drawing**.
    - **Gallery**: Set a photo or a video saved in **Gallery** as a background image.
    - **Camera**: Take a photo or record a video and set it as a background image.
    - **Colour**: Select a background colour.
3. Write or draw on the live message screen.

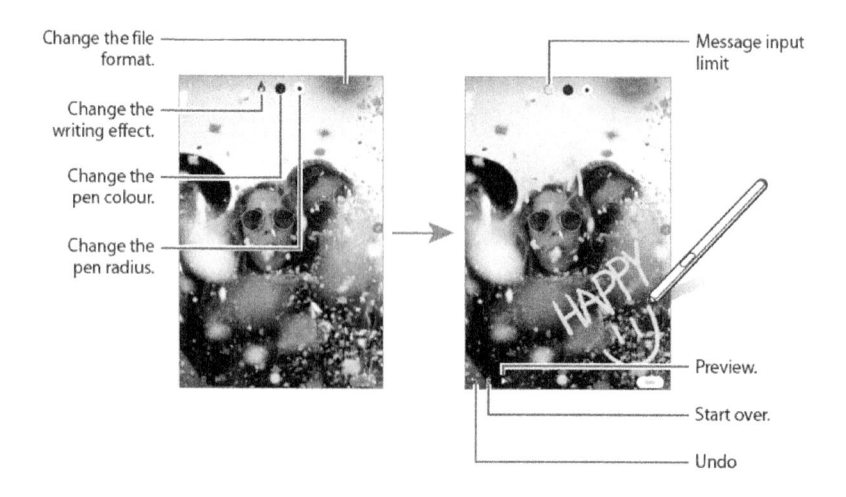

Change the file format.
Change the writing effect.
Change the pen colour.
Change the pen radius.

Message input limit
Preview.
Start over.
Undo

4. Tap **Done**. The live message will be saved in **Gallery** as an animated GIF file or a video.
5. Tap **Share** and select a method.

Bixby Vision

When you hover the S Pen over the content, the content is recognized and available search icons will appear. Use the features to search for similar images, detect and translate text, and more.

1. When there is an image you want to search for relevant information or extract text from, open the Air command panel and tap **Bixby Vision**.
2. Hover the S Pen over the content you want. When the content is recognized, the available search icons will appear.
3. Select an icon you want.
4. To close Bixby Vision, tap ✗ on the Bixby Vision panel.

Screen off memo

You can quickly create memos by writing on the screen without turning on it. If this feature is not activated, launch the **Settings** app, tap **Advanced features**. Select **S Pen** and tap the **Screen off memo** switch to activate it.
To create a screen off memo, follow the steps below.

1. When the screen is off, detach the S Pen or hover the S Pen over the screen and press the S Pen button.
2. Write or draw a memo.

To save the memo, tap **Save** or reattach the S Pen to the S Pen's charging groove. The memo will be saved to **Samsung Notes**.

25

Unlocking the screen using the S Pen

If the screen is locked while the S Pen is connected, you can unlock the screen by pressing the S Pen button. The **Unlock with S Pen remote** feature must bet set as the screen lock method in the following ways.

1. To set this feature, the S Pen must be connected to your device before launching the **Settings** app.
2. Tap **Advanced features** and select **S Pen**
3. Tap **Unlock with S Pen remote** and select **OK**.
4. Unlock the screen using the preset screen lock method. Now you can unlock the screen by pressing the S Pen button.

BIXBY

Bixby is a user interface that helps you use your device more conveniently. You can talk to Bixby or type text. Bixby will launch a function you request or show the information you want. It also learns your usage patterns and environments. The more it learns about you, the more precisely it will understand you. To use Bixby, your device must be connected to a Wi-Fi or mobile network and you must sign in to your Samsung account.

Starting Bixby

When you launch Bixby for the first time, the Bixby intro page will appear. You must select the language to use with Bixby, sign in to your Samsung account according to the on-screen instructions, and then agree to the terms and conditions.

1. Press and hold the Side key. Alternatively, launch the **Bixby** app.

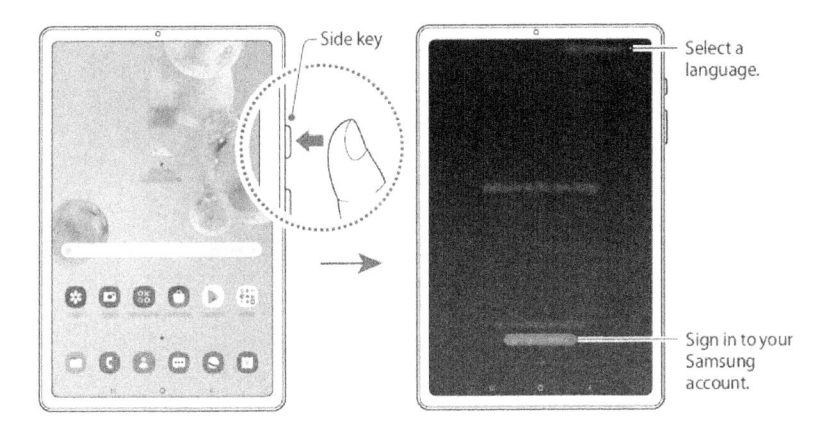

2. Select the language to use with Bixby.
3. Tap **Sign in to Samsung account** and follow the on-screen instructions to sign in to your Samsung account. If you are already signed in, your account information will appear on the screen.
4. Follow the on-screen instructions to complete the setup. The Bixby screen will appear.

Using Bixby

When you say what you want to Bixby, Bixby will launch corresponding functions or show the information you requested. While pressing and holding the Side key, say what you want to Bixby, and release your finger from the key when you are finished speaking. Alternatively, say **Hi, Bixby**, and when the device emits a sound, say what you want.

For example, while pressing and holding the Side key, say **How's the weather today?** The weather information will appear on the screen. If you want to know the weather tomorrow, while pressing and holding the Side key, just say **Tomorrow?** Because Bixby understands the context of the conversation, it will show you tomorrow's weather.

Listening   Corresponding function

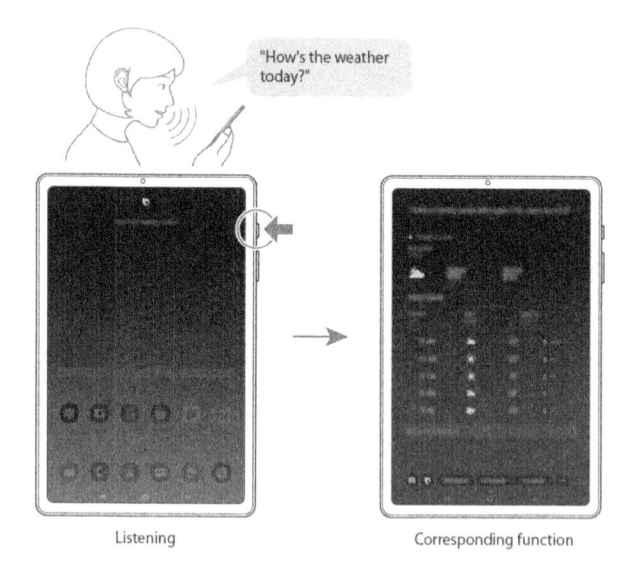

If Bixby asks you a question during a conversation, while pressing and holding the Side key, answer Bixby. Or, tap ⓑ and answer Bixby.

If you are using headphones or Bluetooth audio, or start a conversation by saying **Hi, Bixby**, you can continue the conversation without tapping the icon by following the steps below.

1. Launch the **Bixby** app and tap ⋮
2. Click **Settings** and select **Automatic listening**.
3. Select **Hands-free** only.

Waking up Bixby using your voice

You can start a conversation with Bixby by saying **Hi, Bixby**. Register your voice so that Bixby will respond to your voice when you say **Hi, Bixby**.

1. Launch the **Bixby** app and tap ⋮
2. Click **Settings** and select **Voice wake-up**.
3. Tap the Wake with **Hi, Bixby** switch to activate it.
4. Follow the on-screen instructions to complete the setup.

Now you can say **Hi, Bixby**, and when the device emits a sound, start a conversation.

Communicating by typing text

If your voice is not recognized due to noisy environments or if you are in a situation where speaking is difficult, you can communicate with Bixby via text.

Launch the **Bixby** app, tap 🔲 and then type what you want. During the communication, Bixby also will answer you through text instead of voice feedback.

PHONE

Making voice and video calls

1. Launch the **Phone** app and tap **Keypad**.
2. Enter a phone number.
3. Tap 📞 to make a voice call, or tap 📹 to make a video call.

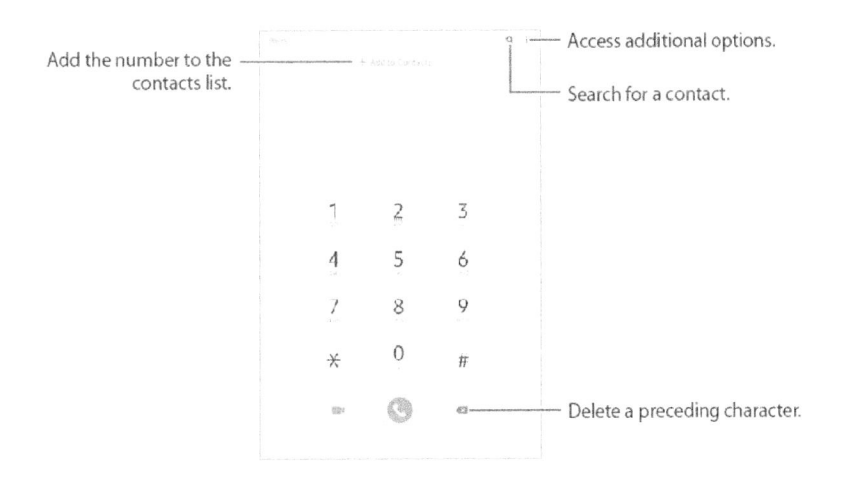

- Add the number to the contacts list.
- Access additional options.
- Search for a contact.
- Delete a preceding character.

Making calls from call logs or contacts list

Launch the Phone app, tap **Recents** or **Contacts**, and then swipe to the right on a contact or a phone number to make a call. If this feature is deactivated, launch the **Settings** app, tap **Advanced features** and select **Motions and gestures** and then tap the **Swipe to call or send messages** switch to activate it.

Using speed dial

Set speed dial numbers to quickly make calls.

To set a number to speed dial, launch the **Phone** app, tap **Keypad** or **Contacts** and click on   to select **Speed dial numbers**, select a speed dial number, and then add a phone number. To make a call, tap and hold a speed dial number on the keypad. For speed dial numbers 10 and up, tap the first digit(s) of the number, and then tap and hold the last digit. For example, if you set the number 123 as a speed dial number, tap 1, tap 2, and then tap and hold 3.

Answering a call

When a call comes in, drag   outside the large circle.

Rejecting a call

When a call comes in, drag   outside the large circle.

To send a message when rejecting an incoming call, drag the **Send message** bar upwards and select a message to send. To create various rejection messages, launch the **Phone** app, tap   and click **Settings**. Then select **Quick decline messages**, enter a message, and then tap

Missed calls

If a call is missed, the ☎ icon appears on the status bar. Open the notification panel to view the list of missed calls. Alternatively, launch the **Phone** app and tap **Recents** to view missed calls.

Blocking phone numbers

Block calls from specific numbers added to your block list.

1. Launch the **Phone** app and tap ⋮
2. Tap **Settings** and select **Blocked numbers**.
3. Tap **Recents** or **Contacts**, select contacts or phone numbers, and then tap **Done**.

When blocked numbers try to contact you, you will not receive notifications. The calls will be logged in the call log.

Options during a voice call

The following actions are available:

- ⋮ : Access additional options.
- **Add call**: Dial a second call. The first call will be put on hold. When you end the second call, the first call will be resumed.
- **Message**: Send a message to the caller.
- **Bluetooth**: Switch to a Bluetooth headset if it is connected to the device.
- **Hold call**: Hold a call. Tap Resume call to retrieve the held call.
- **Mute**: Turn off the microphone so that the other party cannot hear you.
- **Keypad / Hide**: Open or close the keypad.
- ⌒ : End the current call.

Options during a video call

Tap the screen to use the following options:

- ⋮ : Access additional options.
- **Camera**: Turn off the camera so that the other party cannot see you.
- **Switch**: Switch between the front and rear cameras.
- : End the current call.
- **Mute**: Turn off the microphone so that the other party cannot hear you.
- **Bluetooth**: Switch to a Bluetooth headset if it is connected to the device.

Adding a phone number to Contacts from the keypad

1. Launch the **Phone** app and tap **Keypad**.
2. Enter the number.
3. Tap **Add to Contacts**.
4. Tap **Create contact** to create a new contact, or tap **Update existing** to add the number to an existing contact.

Adding a phone number to Contacts from the calls list

1. Launch the **Phone** app and tap **Recents**.
2. Tap a phone number and tap **Add**.
3. Tap **Create contact** to create a new contact, or tap **Update existing** to add the number to an existing contact.

Adding a tag to a phone number

You can add tags to numbers without saving them to Contacts. This allows you to view the caller's information when they call without having them listed in Contacts.

1. Launch the **Phone** app and tap **Recents**.
2. Tap a phone number.
3. Tap **Add tag**, enter a tag, and then tap **Add**. When a call comes from that number, the tag will show under the number.

CREATING AND MANAGING CONTACTS ON THE DEVICE

Creating a new contact

1. Launch the **Contacts** app and tap
2. Select a storage location and tap Select.
3. Enter contact information.

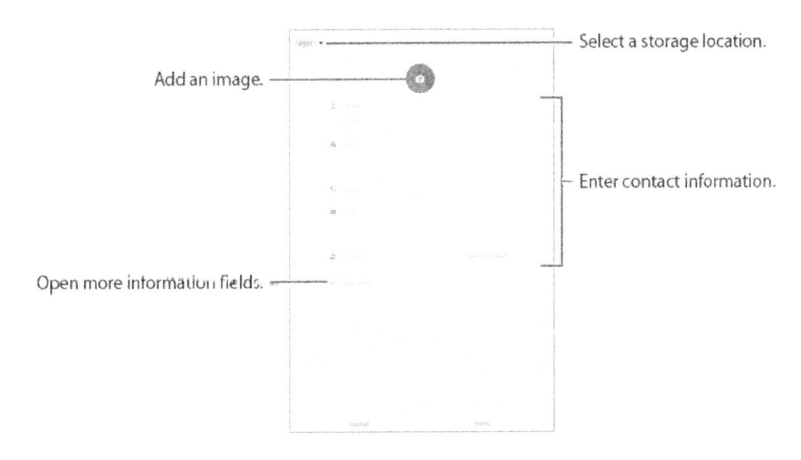

4. Tap **Save**.

Importing contacts

Add contacts by importing them from other storages to your device.

1. Launch the **Contacts** app and tap ≡
2. Tap **Manage contacts** and **select Import/export contacts**.
3. Tap **Import** and Select a storage location to import contacts from.
4. Tick VCF files or contacts to import and tap **Done**.
5. Select a storage location to save contacts to and tap **Import**.

Syncing contacts with your web accounts

Sync your device contacts with online contacts saved in your web accounts, such as your Samsung account.

1. Launch the **Settings** app, tap **Accounts and backup**
2. Tap **Accounts**, and then select the account to sync with.
3. Tap **Sync account** and tap the **Contacts** switch to activate it.

Deleting contacts

1. Launch the **Contacts** app, tap ⋮ at the top of the contacts list, and then tap **Delete**.
2. Select contact(s) and tap **Delete**.

MESSAGES

Sending messages

1. Launch the **Messages** app and tap .
2. Add recipients and enter a message.

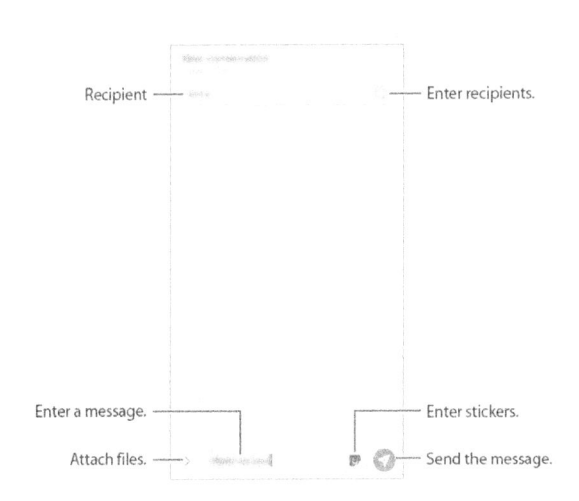

Recipient — Enter recipients.

Enter a message. — Enter stickers.
Attach files. — Send the message.

3. Tap to send the message.

Blocking unwanted messages

Block messages from specific numbers added to your block list.

1. Launch the **Messages** app, tap at the top of the messages list, and then tap **Settings**
2. Select **Block numbers and messages** and tap **Block numbers**.
3. Tap **Inbox** and select a contact or a phone number. Or, tap **Contacts**, select contacts, and then tap **Done**.

Deleting messages

1. Launch the **Messages** app.
2. On the messages list, select a contact or a phone number.
3. Tap and hold a message, then tap **Delete**.

To delete multiple messages, tick messages you want to delete and tap **Delete**.

INTERNET

Browsing webpages

Browse the Internet to search for information and bookmark your favourite webpages to access them conveniently.

1. Launch the **Internet** app.
2. Tap the address field.
3. Enter the web address or a keyword, and then tap **Go**.

Browsing webpages using secret mode

In secret mode, you can separately manage open tabs, bookmarks, and saved pages. You can lock secret mode using a password and your biometric data.

Activating secret mode

Tap ☰ and select **Turn on Secret mode**. If you are using this feature for the first time, set whether to use a password for secret mode. In secret mode, the device will change the colour of the toolbars.

Changing security settings

You can change your password in the following way.

1. Tap ☰ and select **Settings**.
2. Click **Privacy and security**, tap **Secret mode settings** and select **Change password**.

To use your registered biometric data as a lock method along with the password, tap an option switch under Biometrics to activate it.

Deactivating secret mode

Tap ≡ and select **Turn off Secret mode**.

CAMERA

Taking photos

1. Tap the image on the preview screen where the camera should focus.

    - Spread two fingers apart on the screen to zoom in, and pinch to zoom out. Alternatively, drag the lens selection icon to the left or right. Zooming features are available only when using the rear camera.
    - To adjust the brightness of photos, tap the screen. When the adjustment bar appears, drag 💡 on the adjustment bar towards ➕ or ➖.

2. Tap ◯ to take a photo.

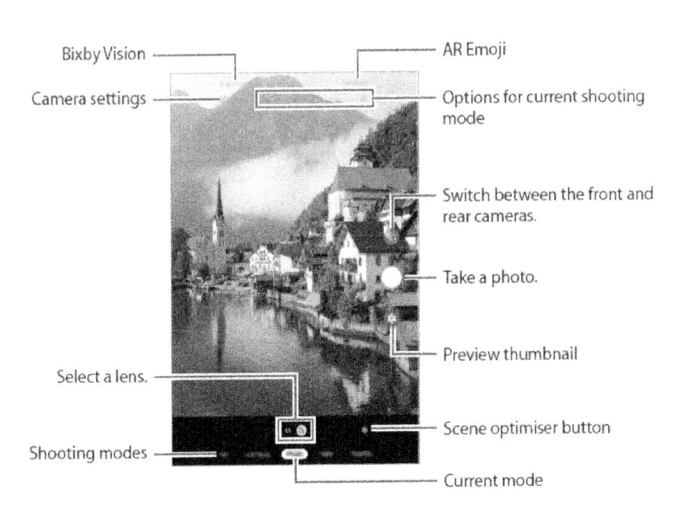

```
Bixby Vision ─────────────        ───── AR Emoji
Camera settings ──────             ───── Options for current shooting
                                          mode
                                   ───── Switch between the front and
                                          rear cameras.
                                   ───── Take a photo.
                                   ───── Preview thumbnail
Select a lens. ──────
                                   ───── Scene optimiser button
Shooting modes ──────
                                   ───── Current mode
```

Selecting a lens for shooting

On the preview screen, tap **Photo**, **Video** or **Panorama**, select the lens you want, and then take a photo or record a video.

- ⌀ The Ultra wide lens lets you take wide-angle photos or record wide-angle videos which look just like the actual view. Use this feature to take landscape photos. To correct the distortion in photos taken with the Ultra wide lens, tap ⚙ on the preview screen, tap **Save options**, and then tap the **Ultra wide lens correction** switch to activate it.

- ⌀ : The wide-angle lens lets you take basic photos or record normal videos.

⌀ Ultra wide shooting   ⌀ Basic shooting

Taking selfies

You can take self-portraits with the front camera.
1. On the shooting modes list, tap **Photo**.
2. On the preview screen, swipe upwards or downwards, or tap 📷 to switch to the front camera for self-portraits.

38

3. Face the front camera lens. To take self-portraits with a wide-angle shot of the landscape or people, tap .
4. Tap ◯ to take a photo.

Video mode

The camera adjusts the shooting options automatically depending on the surroundings to record videos easily.

1. On the shooting modes list, tap **Video**.
2. Tap ⦿ to record a video. To capture an image from the video while recording, tap .
3. Tap ⦿ to stop recording the video.

GALLERY

Viewing images

1. Launch the **Gallery** app and tap **Pictures**.
2. Select an image.

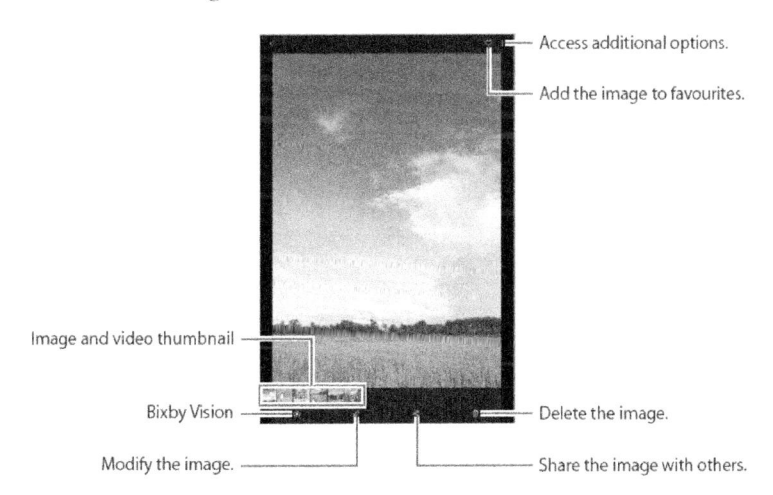

- Access additional options.
- Add the image to favourites.
- Image and video thumbnail
- Bixby Vision
- Modify the image.
- Delete the image.
- Share the image with others.

Viewing videos

1. Launch the **Gallery** app and tap **Pictures**.
2. Select a video to play.
3. Tap **Play video** to play the video.

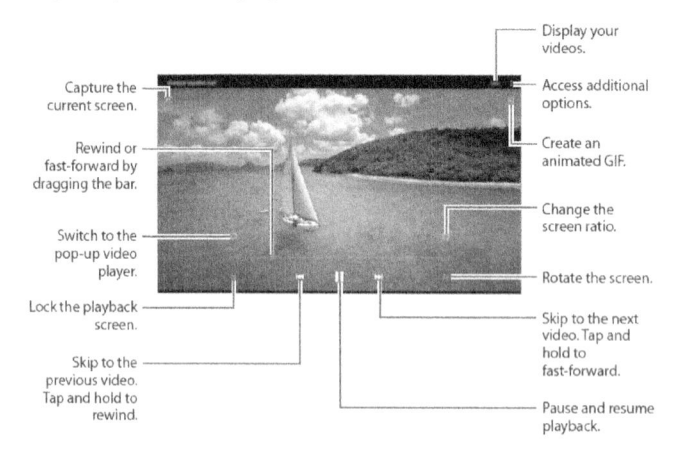

```
Capture the current screen.
Rewind or fast-forward by dragging the bar.
Switch to the pop-up video player.
Lock the playback screen.
Skip to the previous video. Tap and hold to rewind.

Display your videos.
Access additional options.
Create an animated GIF.
Change the screen ratio.
Rotate the screen.
Skip to the next video. Tap and hold to fast-forward.
Pause and resume playback.
```

Drag your finger up or down on the left side of the playback screen to adjust the brightness, or drag your finger up or down on the right side of the playback screen to adjust the volume. To rewind or fast-forward, swipe to the left or right on the playback screen.

Deleting images or videos

1. Launch the **Gallery** app.
2. Select an image or a video to delete. To delete multiple files, tap and hold a file to delete on the list and tick more files to delete.
3. Tap **Delete**.

Using the recycle bin feature

You can keep the deleted images and videos in the recycle bin. The files will be deleted after a certain period.

To activate the recycle bin

1. Launch the **Gallery** app and tap ⋮.
2. Tap **Settings** and select the **Recycle bin** switch to activate it.
3. To view files in the recycle bin
4. Launch the **Gallery** app, tap ⋮ and select **Recycle bin**.

MULTI WINDOW

There are times you wish you had two tablets - that way, you could send an email on one but read an article on another. With split screen view, you can do that with just one tablet. This feature lets you open two apps on your tablet and use them simultaneously, so you can multitask more easily and faster than ever. You can also run multiple apps at the same time in the pop-up view.

Split screen view    Pop-up view

Split screen view
1. Tap the **Recents** button to open the list of recently used apps.
2. Swipe to the left or right, tap an app's icon, and then tap **Open in split screen view**. The selected app will launch in the upper window.

3. On the lower window, swipe left or right to select another app to launch. To launch apps not on the list of recently used apps, tap the **Home** button or **Back** button and select an app.

Pop-up view

1. Tap the **Recents** button to open the list of recently used apps.
2. Swipe to the left or right, tap an app's icon, and then tap **Open in pop-up view**. The app screen will appear in the pop-up view.

Using the Multi window tray

You can quickly access the apps that you want to run in the split screen view.

1. Swipe to the left on the screen.

If the Multi window tray does not appear, launch the **Settings** app, tap **Advanced features**, and then tap the **Multi window tray** switch to activate it.

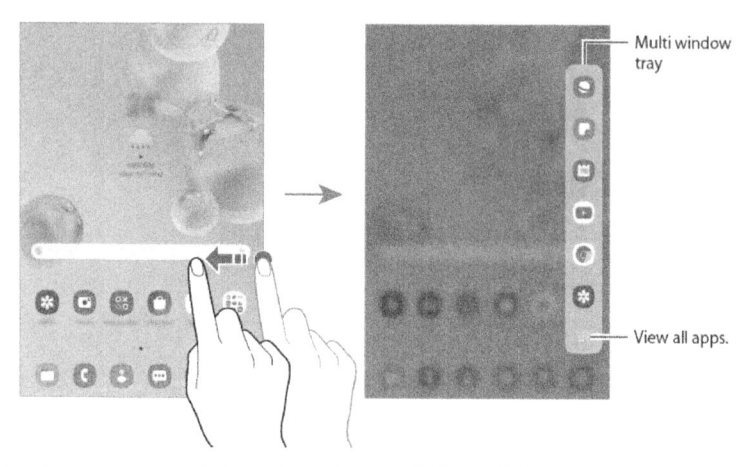

2. Select an app. The selected app will launch in the upper window.
3. Select another app to launch in the lower window.

SAMSUNG NOTES

Creating notes

Create notes by entering text from the keyboard or by handwriting or drawing on the screen. You can also insert images or voice recordings into your notes.

1. Launch the **Samsung Notes** app and tap
2. Select an input method from the toolbar at the top of the screen and compose a note.

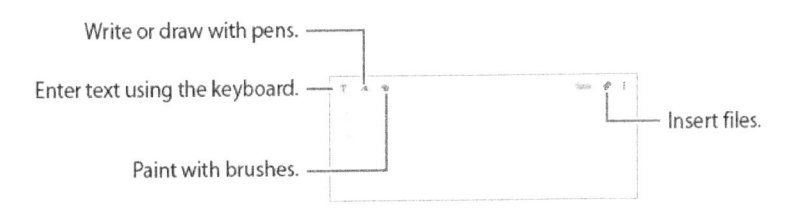

```
Write or draw with pens.
Enter text using the keyboard.
                                                    Insert files.
Paint with brushes.
```

3. When you are finished composing the note, tap **Save**.

Write or draw with pens

This entails composing notes with handwriting using the S Pen. On the note composer screen, tap to write or draw with the S Pen. You can enter your handwriting more easily if you magnify the screen by spreading two fingers on it.

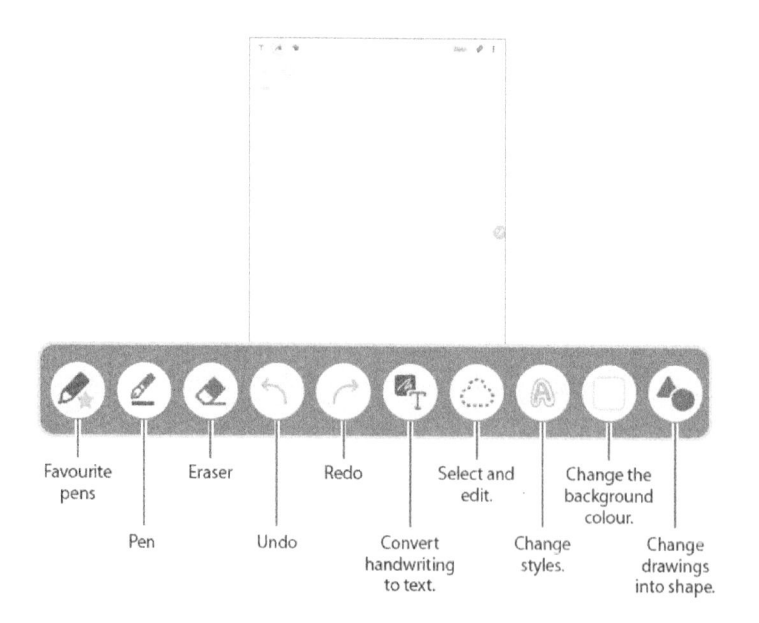

| Favourite pens | Eraser | Redo | Select and edit. | Change the background colour. |
| Pen | Undo | Convert handwriting to text. | Change styles. | Change drawings into shape. |

Editing handwritten notes

Edit handwritten notes using various editing options, such as cutting, moving, resizing, or transforming.

1. When there is handwriting on the note, tap

To change the shape of the selection, tap once more.

2. Tap or draw a line around the input to select.

To move the input to another location, select the input, and then drag it to a new location.

To change the size of the selection, tap the input and drag a corner of the frame that appears.

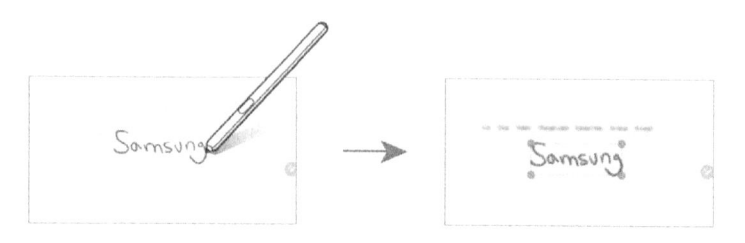

3. Edit the input using the available options.

- **Cut**: Cut out the input. To paste it to another location, tap and hold the location, and then tap **Paste**.
- **Copy**: Copy the input. To paste it to another location, tap and hold the location, and then tap **Paste**.
- **Delete**: Delete the input.
- **Change style**: Change styles. Select a colour or line thickness and tap **Done**.
- **Extract text**: Extract text from the selected area. To paste or copy the text to a note, tap **Paste** or **Copy**.
- **To front**: Send the input to the front.
- **To back**: Send the input to the back.

Changing drawings into shape

You can change your drawings into shapes. Tap and draw. Your drawings will now automatically change into the corresponding shape.

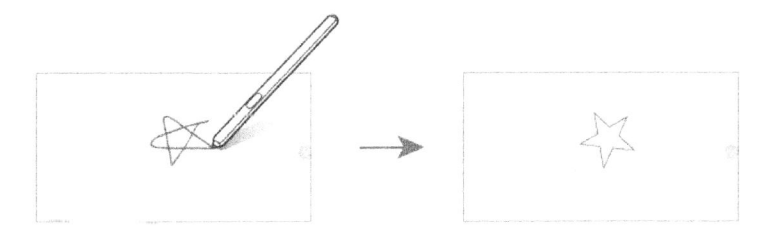

Converting handwriting to text

After writing on the screen, tap it with your finger. To select all of your handwriting, tap . Options will appear in the preview window.

To replace the handwriting with the text, tap **Convert**.

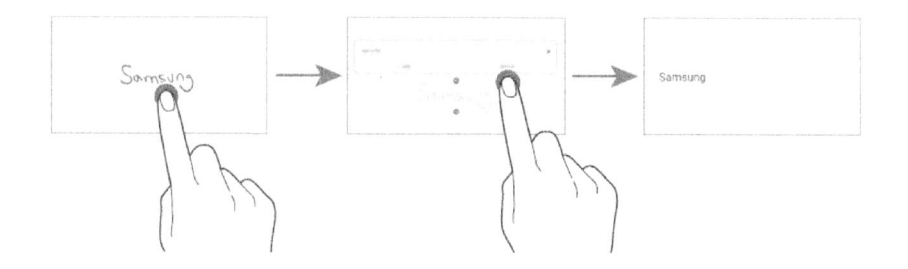

Deleting notes

1. Launch the **Samsung Notes** app.
2. Tap and hold a note to delete. To delete multiple notes, tick more notes to delete.
3. Tap **Delete**.

SAMSUNG FLOW

Samsung Flow allows you to easily connect your tablet to your smartphone and use them conveniently, such as checking notifications or sharing contents. Samsung Flow must be installed on both devices that you want to connect. If Samsung Flow is not installed, download it from **Galaxy Store** or **Play Store**.

Connecting your tablet and smartphone

1. On your smartphone, launch **Samsung Flow**.
2. On your tablet, launch the **Samsung Flow** app.
3. Select your smartphone from the detected devices list.
4. Accept the connection request on both devices.
5. Confirm the passkey on both devices. The devices will be connected.

MY FILES

Access and manage various files stored in the device or in other locations, such as cloud storage services.

Launch the **My Files** app. View files that are stored in each storage.

SMARTTHINGS

Galaxy Tab S6 can control and manage smart appliances and Internet of Things (IoT) products using SmartThings. To use SmartThings, your tablet and other devices must be connected to a Wi-Fi or mobile network. To fully use SmartThings, you must sign in to your Samsung account.

Connecting to nearby devices

Connect to nearby devices, such as Bluetooth headsets, easily and quickly.

1. Launch the **SmartThings** app.
2. Tap **Add device** or tap ✚ and select **Add device**.
3. Tap **Scan**.
4. Select a device from the list and connect to it by following the on-screen instructions.

Registering and controlling home appliances, TVs, and IoT products

Register smart refrigerators, washers, air conditioners, air purifiers, TVs, and Internet of Things (IoT) products on your Galaxy Tab S6, and view their status or control them from your tablet's screen. You can also group devices by location and add rules to control the devices easily and conveniently.

Connecting devices
1. Launch the **SmartThings** app.
2. Tap **Add device** or tap ✚ and select **Add device**.
3. Select a device type or tap **Scan** or **Search** for the devices.
4. Follow the on-screen instructions to connect devices.

Viewing and controlling connected devices
You can view and control the devices. For example, you can adjust the TV volume.
1. Launch the **SmartThings** app. The list of connected devices will appear.
2. View the status of devices on the list.

To control the devices, select a device. When the device controller supplied with the selected device is downloaded, you can control the device.

Adding devices and scenes by locations
You can add devices by locations, view the list of devices in a same location, and control them. You can also add a scene to a location to control multiple devices at the same time.

Adding locations
1. Launch the **SmartThings** app and tap ≡
2. Tap ⌄ and select **Add new location**.
3. Enter the location name.
   To set a location, tap **Geolocation** to select a location on the map and tap **Done**.
   To add rooms to the location, tap **Rooms**, tick rooms you want to add, and then tap **Done**.
4. Tap **Done**. Your location will be added.

To add devices to the location, tap **Add device** or tap ➕ and select **Add device** and follow the on-screen instructions to register devices.

Adding scenes

Add a scene and register devices to it to control multiple devices at the same time.

1. Launch the **SmartThings** app and tap ≡
2. Tap ⌄ and select a location.
3. Tap ≡ and click **Scenes**
4. Select **Add scene** and enter the scene name.
5. Tap ⊕ under **Actions** to add actions to perform and tap **Save**.
6. Tap **Save**.

Adding automations

You can also use your Galaxy Tab S6 to set an automation to operate devices automatically depending on the preset time, the status of devices, and more. For example, add an automation to turn on the audio automatically every day at 7:00 AM.

1. Launch the **SmartThings** app and tap ≡
2. Tap ⌄ and select a location.
3. Tap ≡ and click **Automations**.
4. Select **Add automation** and tap **Custom automation**.
5. Tap ⊕ under **If** and set the activation conditions for the automation, and then tap **Next**.
6. Tap ⊕ under **Then** and set actions to perform, and then tap **Done**.
7. Enter the automation name and tap **OK**.

Receiving notifications

You can receive notifications from connected devices on your tablet. For example, when the laundry is finished, you can receive a notification on your tablet.

To set devices to receive notifications

1. Launch the **SmartThings** app, tap ≡.
2. Tap ⚙ and select **Notifications** and tap the switches next to the devices you want.

SAMSUNG DEX

Samsung DeX is a service that allows you to use your tablet like a computer from tablet screen or an external display, such as a TV or monitor. While using Samsung DeX on external display, you can simultaneously use your tablet. You can connect your tablet to the Keyboard Cover or external display using an HDMI adaptor (USB Type-C to HDMI).

On tablet screen On external display

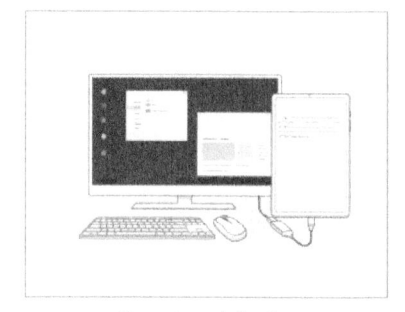

Connecting to the Keyboard Cover

Use your tablet like a computer by connecting the Keyboard Cover. Gently press the device until the device's keyboard dock port connects with the connector of the Keyboard Cover. Samsung DeX screen will appear.

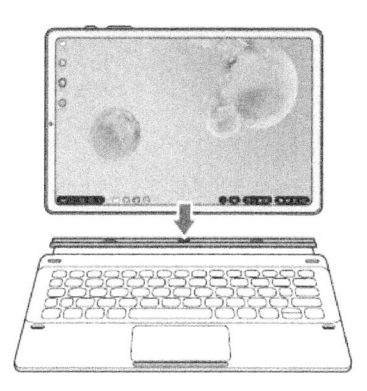

To set the device to switch to Samsung DeX automatically when connecting the Keyboard Cover, launch the **Settings** app, tap **Advanced features** and select **Samsung DeX**, and then tap the **Auto start when Book Cover Keyboard is connected** switch to activate it.

While using the Keyboard Cover, you can easily launch Samsung DeX with a simple key combination (**Fn** + **DeX**).

You can also launch Samsung DeX from quick settings without Keyboard Cover. Swipe downwards on the notification panel and tap **Samsung DeX**.

To use the device upright, attach the backside of the Keyboard Cover to the back of the device.

Connecting to an external display

You can connect your tablet to an external display using an HDMI adaptor.

1. Connect an HDMI adaptor to your tablet.
2. Connect an HDMI cable to the HDMI adaptor and to a TV or monitor's HDMI port.
3. On your tablet's screen, tap **Continue** and select **Start**. Without changing your tablet's screen, the Samsung DeX screen will appear on the connected TV or monitor.

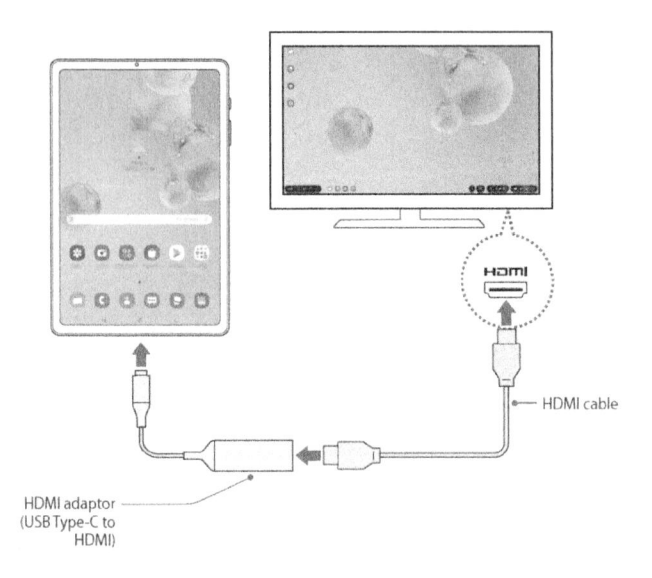

To switch to Samsung DeX directly when connecting the HDMI adaptor, launch the **Settings** app, tap **Advanced features** and select **Samsung DeX** and then tap the **Auto start when HDMI is connected** switch to activate it.

Using Samsung DeX

Use your tablet's features in an interface environment similar to a computer. You can multitask by running multiple apps simultaneously. You can also check your tablet's notifications and status.

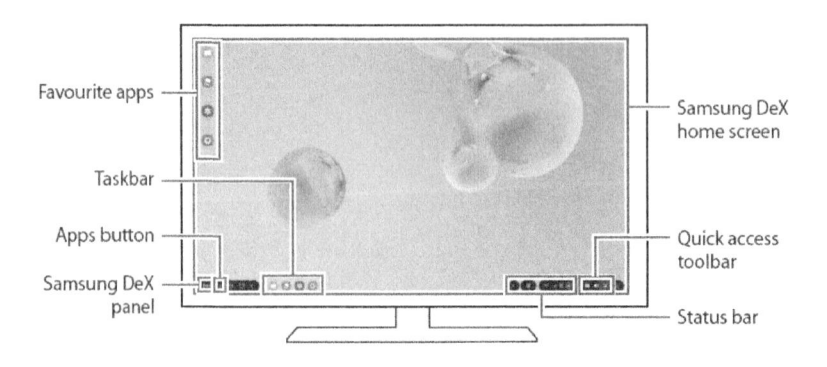

To adjust the screen settings, use the connected TV or monitor's display settings.

Sound will be played through the tablet's speaker. To change the default audio output, launch the **Settings** app, tap **Advanced features**, click on **Samsung DeX**, and then select the **Set default audio output** switch to activate it.

- Favourite apps: Add frequently used apps to the Home screen and launch them quickly.
- Samsung DeX panel: You can use various useful features, such as locking the Samsung DeX screen and viewing how to use Samsung DeX.
- Apps button: View and run your tablet's apps.
- Taskbar: View the apps that are currently running.
- Status bar: View your tablet's notifications and status.
- Quick access toolbar: Use quick tools, such as screen keyboard, volume control, or search.

Ending Samsung DeX

Use the following methods to end Samsung DeX.

1. Press the key combination (**Fn** + **DeX**) when you use Samsung DeX with the Keyboard Cover.
2. Tap **DeX** at the bottom of the left corner and tap Exit DeX.
3. Disconnect your tablet from the HDMI adaptor.

SETTINGS

CONNECTIONS

Change settings for various connections, such as the Wi-Fi feature and Bluetooth.

Wi-Fi

Activate the Wi-Fi feature to connect to a Wi-Fi network and access the Internet or other network devices.

Connecting to a Wi-Fi network

1. On the Settings screen, tap **Connections**, select **Wi-Fi** and tap the switch to activate it.
2. Select a network from the Wi-Fi networks list. Networks that require a password appear with a lock icon. Enter the password and tap **Connect**.
3. Once the device connects to a Wi-Fi network, the device will reconnect to that network each time it is available without requiring a password. To prevent the device connecting to the network automatically, select it from the list of networks and tap **Forget**.

Wi-Fi Direct

Wi-Fi Direct connects devices directly via a Wi-Fi network without requiring an access point.

1. On the Settings screen, tap **Connections**, select **Wi-Fi** and tap the switch to activate it.
2. Tap **Wi-Fi Direct**. The detected devices are listed but if the device you want to connect to is not in the list, request that the device turns on its Wi-Fi Direct feature.
3. Select a device to connect to. The devices will be connected when the other device accepts the Wi-Fi Direct connection request.

Sending and receiving data

You can share data, such as contacts or media files, with other devices. The following actions are an example of sending an image to another device.

1. Launch the **Gallery** app and select an image.
2. Tap , select **Wi-Fi Direct** and select a device to transfer the image to.
3. Accept the Wi-Fi Direct connection request on the other device. If the devices are already connected, the image will be sent to the other device without the connection request procedure.

Ending the device connection

1. On the Settings screen, tap **Connections** and select **Wi-Fi**.
2. Tap **Wi-Fi Direct**. The device displays the connected devices in the list.
3. Tap the device name to disconnect the devices.

Bluetooth

Use Bluetooth to exchange data or media files with other Bluetooth-enabled devices.

Pairing with other Bluetooth devices

1. On the Settings screen, tap **Connections**, select **Bluetooth** and tap the switch to activate it. The detected devices will be listed.
2. Select a device to pair with. If the device you want to pair with is not on the list, set the device to enter Bluetooth pairing mode.
3. Accept the Bluetooth connection request on your device to confirm. The devices will be connected when the other device accepts the Bluetooth connection request.

55

Sending and receiving data

Many apps support data transfer via Bluetooth. You can share data, such as contacts or media files, with other Bluetooth devices. The following actions are an example of sending an image to another device.

1. Launch the **Gallery** app and select an image.
2. Tap select **Bluetooth** and select a device to transfer the image to. If the device you want to pair with is not in the list, request that the device turns on its visibility option.
3. Accept the Bluetooth connection request on the other device.

Dual audio

You can connect up to two Bluetooth audio devices to your tablet. Connect two Bluetooth headsets or speakers to use them at the same time.

1. On the Settings screen, tap **Connections**, select **Bluetooth** and tap the switch to activate it. The detected devices will be listed.
2. Tap , select **Advanced**, tap the **Dual audio** switch to activate it, and then tap the **Back** button.
3. Select a device to pair with. If the device you want to pair with is not in the list, turn on its visibility option or enter Bluetooth pairing mode on the device.
4. Tap next to the connected device and tap the **Audio** switch to activate it.
5. Select another device from the list and activate its **Audio** feature.

Unpairing Bluetooth devices

1. On the Settings screen, tap **Connections** and select **Bluetooth**. The device displays the paired devices in the list.
2. Tap next to the device name to unpair.

3. Tap **Unpair**.

Mobile Hotspot and Tethering

Use the device as a mobile hotspot to share the device's mobile data connection with other devices when the network connection is not available. Connections can be made via Wi-Fi, USB, or Bluetooth.

Using the mobile hotspot

Use your device as a mobile hotspot to share your device's mobile data connection with other devices.

1. On the Settings screen, tap **Connections**, select **Mobile Hotspot and Tethering**; and **tap Mobile Hotspot**.
2. Tap the switch to activate it. The icon appears on the status bar. Other devices can find your device in the Wi-Fi networks list.
   To set a password for the mobile hotspot, tap ⋮ and click **Configure Mobile Hotspot** and select the level of security. Then, enter a password and tap **Save**.
3. On the other device's screen, search for and select your device from the Wi-Fi networks list.
4. On the connected device, use the device's mobile data connection to access the Internet.

PRINTING

Configure settings for printer plug-ins installed on the device. You can connect the device to a printer via Wi-Fi or Wi-Fi Direct, and print images or documents.

Adding printer plug-ins

Add printer plug-ins for printers you want to connect the device to.

1. On the Settings screen, tap **Connections** and select **More connection settings**.
2. Tap **Printing** and select **Download plugin**.
3. Search for a printer plug-in in **Play Store**.
4. Select a printer plug-in and install it.
5. Select the installed printer plug-in. The device will automatically search for printers that are connected to the same Wi-Fi network as your device.
6. Select a printer to add.

You can manually add printers in the following way.

Tap ⋮ and select **Add printer**.

Printing content

While viewing content, such as images or documents, access the options list, tap **Print** and click ▼. Select **All printers...**, and then select a printer.

DISPLAY

Change the display and the Home screen settings.

Blue light filter

Reduce eye strain by limiting the amount of blue light emitted by the screen.

1. On the Settings screen, tap **Display**, select **Blue light filter** and tap the **Turn on now** switch to activate it.
2. Drag the adjustment bar to adjust the filter's opacity.

3. To set the schedule to apply the blue light filter to the screen, tap the **Turn on as scheduled** switch to activate it and select an option.

- **Sunset to sunrise**: Set the device to apply the blue light filter at night and turn it off in the morning based on your current location.
- **Custom schedule**: Set a specific time to apply the blue light filter.

Night mode

Reduce eye strain by applying the dark theme when using the device at night or in a dark place.

1. On the Settings screen, tap **Display**, select **Night mode** and tap the **Turn on now** switch to activate it.
2. To set the schedule to apply night mode to the screen, tap the **Turn on as scheduled** switch to activate it and select an option.

- **Sunset to sunrise**: Set the device to turn on night mode at night and turn it off in the morning based on your current location.
- **Custom schedule**: Set a specific time to turn on and off night mode.

Screensaver

You can set to display images as a screensaver when the screen turns off automatically. The screensaver will be displayed when the device is charging.

1. On the Settings screen, tap **Display**, select **Screensaver** and tap the switch to activate it.

2. Select an option. If you select **Photo Frame** or **Photos**, a slideshow with selected images will start. If you select **Photo Table**, selected images will appear as small cards and overlap.
3. Tap ⚙ to select albums for displaying images.
4. When you are finished, tap the Back button. To preview the selected option, tap **Preview**.

LOCK SCREEN

Change the settings for the locked screen.

Smart Lock

You can set the device to unlock itself and remain unlocked when trusted locations or devices are detected. For example, if you have set your home as a trusted location, when you get home your device will detect the location and automatically unlock itself.
1. On the Settings screen, tap **Lock screen** and select **Smart Lock**.
2. Unlock the screen using the preset screen lock method.
3. Select an option and follow the on-screen instructions to complete the setup.

Biometrics and security

Change the settings for securing the device.

Face recognition

You can set the device to unlock the screen by recognizing your face. Before using the face recognition to unlock your device, you must bear in mind that face recognition is less secure than Pattern, PIN, or Password;

and your device could be unlocked by someone or something that looks like your image.

Registering your face

For better face registration, register your face indoors and out of direct sunlight.
1. On the Settings screen, tap **Biometrics and security** and select **Face recognition**.
2. Read the on-screen instructions and tap **Continue**.
3. Set a screen lock method.
4. Select whether you are wearing glasses or not and tap **Continue**.
5. Hold the device with the screen facing towards you and look at the screen.
6. Position your face inside the frame on the screen. The camera will scan your face.

Deleting the registered face data

You can delete face data that you have registered.
1. On the Settings screen, tap **Biometrics and security** and select **Face recognition**.
2. Unlock the screen using the preset screen lock method.
3. Tap **Remove face data** and select **Remove**. Once the registered face is deleted, all the related features will also be deactivated.

Unlocking the screen with your face

You can unlock the screen with your face instead of using a pattern, PIN, or password.
1. On the Settings screen, tap **Biometrics and security** and select **Face recognition**.

2. Unlock the screen using the preset screen lock method.
3. Tap the **Face unlock** switch to activate it.
4. On the locked screen, look at the screen. When your face is recognised, you can unlock the screen without using any additional screen lock method. If your face is not recognised, use the preset screen lock method.

Fingerprint recognition

In order for fingerprint recognition to function, your fingerprint information needs to be registered and stored in your device. After registering, you can set the device to use your fingerprint for the screen lock

Registering fingerprints

1. On the Settings screen, tap **Biometrics and security** and select **Fingerprints**.
2. Read the on-screen instructions and tap **Continue**.
3. Set a screen lock method.
4. Place your finger on the fingerprint recognition sensor at the bottom of the screen. After the device detects your finger, lift it up and place it on the fingerprint recognition sensor again. Repeat this action until the fingerprint is registered.
5. When you are finished registering your fingerprints, tap **Done**.

Checking registered fingerprints

You can check whether your fingerprint is registered by placing your finger on the fingerprint recognition sensor.

1. On the Settings screen, tap **Biometrics and security** and select **Fingerprints**.
2. Unlock the screen using the preset screen lock method.

3. Tap **Check added fingerprints**.
4. Place your finger on the fingerprint recognition sensor. The recognition result will be displayed.

Deleting registered fingerprints

You can delete registered fingerprints.

1. On the Settings screen, tap **Biometrics and security** and select **Fingerprints**.
2. Unlock the screen using the preset screen lock method.
3. Select a fingerprint to delete and tap **Remove**.

Unlocking the screen with your fingerprints

You can unlock the screen with your fingerprint instead of using a pattern, PIN, or password.

1. On the Settings screen, tap **Biometrics and security** and select **Fingerprints**.
2. Unlock the screen using the preset screen lock method.
3. Tap the **Fingerprint unlock** switch to activate it.
4. On the locked screen, place your finger on the fingerprint recognition sensor and scan your fingerprint.

ACCOUNTS AND BACKUP

Sync, back up, or restore your device's data using Samsung Cloud. You can also sign in to accounts, such as your Samsung account or Google account, or transfer data to or from other devices via Smart Switch.

Users

Set up additional user accounts for other users to use the device with personalised settings, such as email accounts, wallpaper preferences, and more. The following types of user accounts are available:

- Administrator: The administrator account is created only when setting up the device for the first time, and cannot be created more than one. This account has full control of the device including user account management. You can add or delete user accounts only when using this account.
- Guest: This account allows guests to access the device. Information and data used during a guest session is temporarily stored. Each time you use this account, you are asked whether to continue the previous guest session or reset it.
- New user: This account allows users to access their own apps and content, and customize the device settings that affect all accounts.
- New restricted account: A restricted account can only access the apps and content allowed by the administrator account, and cannot use the services that require logging in.

Adding users

The available options may vary depending on the device model chosen.

1. On the Settings screen, tap **Accounts and backup** and select **Users**.
2. ▶ **SM-T865**: Tap **Add user**, select **OK** and tap **Set up now**.
   ▶ **SM-T860, SM-T867**: Tap **Add user or profile**, select **User**, tap **OK** and tap **Set up now**.
   The device will switch to a new user account and the default locked screen will appear on the screen.
3. Unlock the device and follow the on-screen instructions to complete the account setup.

Adding restricted profiles (SM-T860, SM-T867)

1. On the Settings screen, tap **Accounts and backup** and select **Users**.
2. Tap **Add user or profile**, select **User (restricted profile)** and tap **Set up screen lock**.

   If you are not using a secure screen lock method with the administrator account, follow the on-screen instructions to set one up.
3. Select the apps and content that restricted users are allowed to access.

Switching users

Tap the user account icon at the top of the locked screen and select an account to switch to.

Locked screen

Samsung Cloud

Sync the data saved in your device with Samsung Cloud and view the data you have saved on Samsung Cloud. You can also back up your device's data to Samsung Cloud and restore it later. It's imperative to note that to use Samsung Cloud, you must sign in to your Samsung account.

Syncing data

You can sync data saved in your device with Samsung Cloud and access it from other devices.

1. On the Settings screen, tap **Accounts and backup** and select **Samsung Cloud**.
2. Tap ⋮ and select **Settings**
3. Tap **Sync and auto backup settings** and select **Sync**.
4. Tap the switches next to the items you want to sync with.

Backing up data

You can back up your device's data to Samsung Cloud.

1. On the Settings screen, tap **Accounts and backup**, select **Samsung Cloud** and tap **Back up this tablet**.
2. Tick items you want to back up and tap **Back up**.
3. Tap **Done**.

Restoring data

You can restore your backup data from Samsung Cloud to your device.

1. On the Settings screen, tap **Accounts and backup** and select **Samsung Cloud**.
2. Tap **Restore data**, click ▼ and select a device you want.
3. Tick items you want to restore and tap **Restore**.

SAMSUNG GALAXY TAB S6 TIPS & TRICKS

Tablets have long been pitched as devices that can help you get work done on the move. The idea has always been to take a tablet where you don't want to be carrying a laptop. The Galaxy Tab S6 has an improved version of DeX which gives the user a laptop-like experience when attached to the new Book Cover keyboard. Here are some of the tips and tricks to enable you get the best out of your Galaxy Tab S6.

Replace the S Pen nibs
If you use your S Pen on a daily basis, its nib can wear out over time. When that happens, you can replace the nib with one of the spare S Pen nibs that came included with your tablet. To replace it, use tweezers to pull out the S Pen's nib. Insert a new nib, and then push it until it clicks in place.

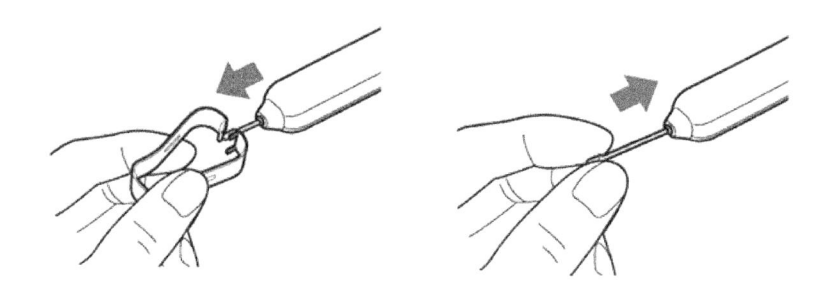

Change Samsung on-screen keyboard settings
Samsung keyboard is the default on-screen keyboard for your tablet. And it can be customized to make it even more useful and convenient. To customize the Samsung keyboard, follow the steps below:
1. Launch **Settings** app and tap **Language and input**.
2. Tap **On-screen keyboard**, and then tap **Samsung Keyboard**.
3. Customize the available settings the way you want them.

Switch keyboard input language

If you're multilingual or learning a new language, you can use more than one language for your on-screen keyboard. But first, you'll need to add the other languages you want to use.

1. Launch **Settings** app and tap **Language and input**.
2. Tap **On-screen keyboard**, and then tap **Samsung Keyboard**.
3. Tap **Languages and types**, and then tap **Manage input languages**.
4. Select or download from the available languages for Samsung keyboard.

To switch the keyboard's input language, open an app that uses the keyboard. Then, swipe the spacebar left or right to switch the language input.

Google voice typing

Google voice lets you type words using only your voice. It's super helpful, especially if your hands are full. To use Google voice type, open an app that uses the keyboard. Then, tap the **Microphone** icon and say what you want to type.

To customize Google voice typing, follow the steps below.

1. Launch **Settings** app and tap **Language and input**.
2. Tap **On-screen keyboard**, and then tap **Google voice typing**.
3. Customize the available settings the way you want them.

Note: This feature is enabled by default and is built into your Samsung keyboard.

Accessibility options on your tablet

Galaxy Tab S6 is meant to be used by everyone. If you have some kind of impairment, you can feel assured that your tablet has built-in Accessibility settings to make it easier to use. You can turn on Voice Assistant for Vision impairments, subtitles for Hearing impairments, and Interaction control for better dexterity and interaction.

Voice Assistant

If you have some trouble reading the text and buttons on your tablet, don't worry. Galaxy Tab s6 comes with Voice Assistant which will read everything you touch. To activate it, follow the steps below:

1. Launch **Settings** app, and select **Accessibility**
2. Tap Screen reader and select **Voice Assistant**.
3. Review permissions, and then tap **Allow**. Some functions may need to be turned off temporarily; tap **OK**.

Note: To turn off Voice Assistant, tap **Voice Assistant** to select it, and then double tap OK.

Hearing enhancements

Subtitles are extremely helpful when you are having difficulty hearing. Your tablet has its very own subtitles for when you're watching a movie or binge-watching your favorite show. To activate hearing enhancement, follow the steps below:

1. Launch **Settings** app and tap **Accessibility**.
2. Select **Hearing enhancements** and tap any of the options: Samsung subtitles (CC) or Google subtitles (CC).

Interactions control

Some people just function better when they use their hands. If you are one of those people, you can set up Interaction control to make controlling your tablet easier. Follow the steps below to activate the interaction control.

1. Launch **Settings** app and tap **Accessibility**.

2. Select **Interaction and dexterity** and tap **Interaction control** to customize the areas of screen interactions, hard keys, and the keyboard.

Assistant Menu

The Assistant Menu is designed for individuals with motor control impairments. When you use the Assistant Menu, you can access physical buttons and all parts of the screen by simply tapping or swiping. Follow the steps below to activate the Assistant menu.

1. Launch **Settings** app and tap **Accessibility**.
2. Select **Interaction and dexterity** and tap **assistant menu** and then tap the switch to the **On** position to start using the Assistant menu.

You can navigate to the Home screen, open recent apps, go back to the previous screen, and more without having to press any physical buttons.

TROUBLESHOOTING PROBLEMS WITH GALAXY TAB S6

Before contacting a service center for repair of your Galaxy Tab S6, here is some of the do-it-yourself troubleshooting guide for solving common issues.

When you turn on your device or while you are using the device, it prompts you to enter one of the following codes:

- Password: When the device lock feature is enabled, you must enter the password you set for the device.
- PIN: When using the device for the first time or when the PIN requirement is enabled, you must enter the PIN supplied with the SIM or USIM card.
- PUK: Your SIM or USIM card is blocked, usually as a result of entering your PIN incorrectly several times. You must enter the PUK supplied by your service provider.
- PIN2: When you access a menu requiring the PIN2, you must enter the PIN2 supplied with the SIM or USIM card.

Your device displays network or service error messages

- When you are in areas with weak signals or poor reception, you may lose reception. Move to another area and try again. While moving, error messages may appear repeatedly
- You cannot access some options without a subscription. For more information, contact your service provider.

Your device does not turn on

When the battery is completely discharged, your device will not turn on. Fully charge the battery before turning on the device.

The touchscreen responds slowly or improperly

- If you attach a screen protector or optional accessories to the touchscreen, the touchscreen may not function properly.
- If you are wearing gloves, if your hands are not clean while touching the touchscreen, or if you tap the screen with sharp objects or your fingertips, the touchscreen may malfunction.
- The touchscreen may malfunction in humid conditions or when exposed to water.
- Restart your device to clear any temporary software bugs.
- Ensure that your device software is updated to the latest version.
- If the touchscreen is scratched or damaged, visit a Samsung Service Centre.

Your device freezes or encounters a fatal error

Try the following solutions. If the problem is still not resolved, contact a service centre.

Restarting the device

If your device freezes or hangs, you may need to close apps or turn off the device and turn it on again.

Forcing restart

If your device is frozen and unresponsive, press and hold the Side key and the Volume Down key simultaneously for more than 7 seconds to restart it.

Resetting the device

If the methods above do not solve your problem, perform a factory data reset.

1. Launch the **Settings** app and tap **General management**.
2. Tap **Reset** and select **Factory data reset**.
3. Tap **Reset** and select **Delete all**.

Before performing the factory data reset, remember to make backup copies of all important data stored in the device.

Calls are not connected

- Ensure that you have accessed the right cellular network.
- Ensure that you have not set call barring for the phone number you are dialing.
- Ensure that you have not set call barring for the incoming phone number.

Others cannot hear you speaking on a call

- Ensure that you are not covering the built-in microphone.
- Ensure that the microphone is close to your mouth.
- If using an earphone, ensure that it is properly connected.

Sound echoes during a call

Adjust the volume by pressing the Volume key or move to another area.

A cellular network or the Internet is often disconnected or audio quality is poor

- Ensure that you are not blocking the device's internal antenna.
- When you are in areas with weak signals or poor reception, you may lose reception. You may have connectivity problems due to issues with the service provider's base station.
- Move to another area and try again.

- When using the device while moving, wireless network services may be disabled due to issues with the service provider's network.

The battery does not charge properly (For Samsung-approved chargers)

- Ensure that the charger is connected properly.
- Visit a Samsung Service Centre and have the battery replaced.

The battery depletes faster than when first purchased

- When you expose the device or the battery to very cold or very hot temperatures, the useful charge may be reduced.
- Battery consumption will increase when you use certain features or apps, such as GPS, games, or the Internet.
- The battery is consumable and the useful charge will get shorter over time.

Error messages appear when launching the camera

Your device must have sufficient available memory and battery power to operate the camera app. If you receive error messages when launching the camera, try the following:

- Charge the battery.
- Free some memory by transferring files to a computer or deleting files from your device.
- Restart the device. If you are still having trouble with the camera app after trying these tips, contact a Samsung Service Centre.

Photo quality is poorer than the preview

- The quality of your photos may vary, depending on the surroundings and the photography techniques you use.
- If you take photos in dark areas, at night, or indoors, image noise may occur or images may be out of focus.

Error messages appear when opening multimedia files

If you receive error messages or multimedia files do not play when you open them on your device, try the following:

- Free some memory by transferring files to a computer or deleting files from your device.
- Ensure that the music file is not Digital Rights Management (DRM)-protected. If the file is DRM-protected, ensure that you have the appropriate licence or key to play the file.
- Ensure that the file formats are supported by the device. If a file format is not supported, such as DivX or AC3, install an app that supports it.
- Your device supports photos and videos captured with the device. Photos and videos captured by other devices may not work properly.
- Your device supports multimedia files that are authorised by your network service provider or providers of additional services. Some content circulated on the Internet, such as ringtones, videos, or wallpapers, may not work properly.

Bluetooth is not working well

- If another Bluetooth device is not located or there are connection problems or performance malfunctions, try the following:

- Ensure that the device you wish to connect with is ready to be scanned or connected to.
- Ensure that your device and the other Bluetooth device are within the maximum Bluetooth range (10 m).
- On your device, launch the **Settings** app, tap **Connections**, and then tap the **Bluetooth** switch to re-activate it.

If the tips above do not solve the problem, contact a Samsung Service Centre.

A connection is not established when you connect the device to a computer

- Ensure that the USB cable you are using is compatible with your device.
- Ensure that you have the proper driver installed and updated on your computer.
- If you are a Windows XP user, ensure that you have Windows XP Service Pack 3 or higher installed on your computer.

Your device cannot find your current location

GPS signals may be obstructed in some locations, such as indoors. Set the device to use Wi-Fi or a mobile network to find your current location in these situations.

The Home button does not appear

The navigation bar containing the Home button may disappear while using certain apps or features. To view the navigation bar, drag upwards from the bottom of the screen.

The screen brightness adjustment bar does not appear on the notification panel

Open the notification panel by dragging the status bar downwards, and then drag the notification panel downwards. Tap ∨ next to the brightness adjustment bar and tap the **Show control on top** switch to activate it.

Printed in Great Britain
by Amazon